FINDING GOD'S FAVOR

GROUP BIBLE STUDY

A Study of Bible Characters
Who Experienced the Favor of God

WRITTEN BY Kevin Stiffler

Finding God's Favor: A Study of Bible Characters Who Experienced the Favor of God
Written by Kevin Stiffler

Requests for information should be sent to:
Warner Press Inc.
P.O. Box 2499
Anderson, IN 46018
www.warnerpress.org

Liz Flinn • Editor
S. Katie Miller • Layout & Design

CONTENTS

Introduction 5

L1 Lesson 1 Noah 9

L2 Lesson 2 Abraham 21

L3 Lesson 3 Moses 31

L4 Lesson 4 Mary 39

L5 Lesson 5 Jesus 49

L6 Lesson 6 Favor versus Favoritism 59

The Warner Press *Relevance* Group Bible Studies provide intriguing examinations of topics using the whole of the Scriptures. The guides incorporate various stories and activities to introduce and apply the subject matter, with a Bible study component at the heart of each session. Our goal is to show life-long believers and those new to the faith how to know the Lord intimately while encouraging them to step out and join him in his work with miraculous results.

These flexible studies are ideal for any setting. We know that time is a valuable commodity in today's society, and that's why each book consists of five or six short lessons intended to meet the group's scheduling needs.

Introduction

One risk in putting together a Bible study on finding God's favor is that it will seem to promote a "prosperity gospel"—that is, the view that God's favor means lots of money and possessions, perfect health, and absolute safety for his children. Another risk is that the study will lead participants to believe in "works-based" salvation and righteousness that are based on somehow "earning" the favor of God by saying and doing the right things. There might even be a risk of some people feeling selfish or self-centered if they desire the favor of God for their lives.

The word *favor* can be understood to mean everything from "friendly regard" shown to someone else (especially by a superior), to approving of a person and his or her actions, to popularity, to a token of love, to a special right or privilege someone has. The dominant Hebrew term from the Old Testament that is translated as "favor" is חֵן (hên), which is also sometimes rendered as "grace." The Greek term from the New Testament is χαριτόω (chhar-i-too—think "charisma"), meaning to bestow or endow with grace.

For each of the characters and stories in this book, the Bible text specifically mentions a person or people finding favor with God or experiencing the favor of God. There are other people in the Bible who enjoyed God's favor. And the Bible contains many, many instances of people who were blessed by God without it being specifically called "favor."

The passages you will study reveal God's favor as it was seen in a variety of situations across the Old and New Testaments. *Bible Backgrounds* by Merle D. Strege (Anderson, IN: Warner Press, 2006) and the series Interpretation: A Bible Commentary for Teaching and Preaching by various authors (Louisville: John Knox Press, various dates) provided valuable insight and perspective for the covered passages.

In response to God's declaration that the Lord would establish King David's throne (the rule of David's descendants) forever, David replied, "Who am I, Sovereign LORD, and what is my family, that you have brought me this far?" (2 Samuel 7:18). David's response to this overwhelming blessing of God was one of deep gratitude. And this is a great place for us to start, with a sense of gratitude to God for his favor.

If it were possible to understand and neatly categorize all there is to know about the favor of God, someone would have already produced a summary that answers everyone's questions. Yet we still explore this topic because God said, "My thoughts are not your thoughts, neither are your ways my ways.... As the heavens are higher than the earth, so are my ways higher than your ways and my thoughts than your thoughts" (Isaiah 55:8–9). The Lord also said, "As the rain and the snow come down from heaven, and do not return to it without watering the earth and making it bud and flourish, so that it yields seed for the sower and bread for the eater, so is my word that goes out from my mouth: It will not return to me empty, but will accomplish what I desire and achieve the purpose for which I sent it" (Isaiah 55:10–11). As we commit ourselves to studying God's Word, it will give us valuable perspective about God's favor.

Noah

Genesis 6

Main Point

As with Noah, our faithfulness to God and his plan can bring God's favor and blessing to others.

Background

Some scholars contend that the first five books of the Bible are the compilation of interpreters and editors of the narratives and oral traditions handed down to them. In Genesis 7:2, for example, we read that God commanded Noah to choose "seven of every kind of clean animal." But Genesis 6:20 and 7:8 both speak of pairs—male and female. What do such discrepancies mean for our faith? The biblical text allows us to watch Israel's faith develop and grow. It is also important, however, that we view the text as we now have it within the canon of the Scriptures. From this broader perspective, such questions as whether Noah chose seven or two of each animal recede into the background as we attend to the great theological themes that command our attention. Yahweh's high hopes for his creation went awry, and the world became something much less than God desired. The narrative of the flood is an indictment of human folly. But it also illustrates Yahweh's will for a new creation, including us.

The Great Flood

The story of the great flood is among the most familiar in the Scriptures. People who cannot recite a single Bible verse still recognize Noah's name. In the hands of ancient Israel's storytellers and poets, this familiar narrative affirms some of the most fundamental theological convictions of Israelite faith. God's creation stubbornly and perversely resisted his purposes. A deep problem had emerged in the relationship between the Lord God and his creation, leading to a significant theological issue concerning life in the company of a holy and righteous God.

Write down your initial understanding of the story of Noah and the flood.

____

____

____

____

What do you think was the basis of the rift between God and his creation? How could this rift have become so wide that God needed to send the flood?

____

____

____

____

I. Read Genesis 6:1–8.

Genesis 6 introduces us to Noah, and it begins with some details that almost seem curious. Scholars are unsure exactly what is meant by "the sons of God" marrying "the daughters of humans" (Genesis 6:2), or just what the Nephilim were (verse 4). As we move on to verse 5, the text stipulates "how great the wickedness of the human race had become." This may imply that the activities described in the previous verses were part of that wickedness. Does it make a difference whether we understand specifically the interaction between "the sons of God" and "the daughters of humans" and the identity of the Nephilim? Why or why not?

What does the activity of God in verse 3 imply about God with respect to human beings?

How might the author of this portion of Genesis have known about God's troubled heart and his regret over making human beings? Did God say so somehow, or was this information divinely revealed? Why do you respond as you do, and what difference does it make?

Why would God determine to wipe out the animals as well as human beings? What does this imply about creation as a whole and our relationship with its other elements?

II. Read Genesis 6:9–22.

God's creation got off to a great start, but then things took a turn. By the time we get to the story of Noah and the flood, there is an apparent trajectory toward judgment and death. But death is not God's last word. Beyond death there is life. How would you summarize and describe the qualities God saw in Noah that made the Lord decide to allow the human race to continue through this one man and his family? What would it mean, practically, to live in these ways?

Genesis 6 describes the people of the earth as being wicked and evil, corrupt and violent. Later, in Genesis 19, we read about God's destruction of the cities of Sodom and Gomorrah because of the "grievous sin" of their people (Genesis 18:20). What specific actions might have caused God to view people in this way? How prevalent must this behavior have been, and why? Describe how, in your opinion, it might compare to the wickedness, evil, corruption, and violence in the world today.

Why do you think the Bible provides such intricate detail about God's instructions for building the ark—the wood to be used, the finish on the outside, the dimensions and the openings?

At this point, the story of Noah does not tell us anything about the righteousness of Noah's wife and sons—only that of Noah. Yet the ark bore eight humans—Noah and his wife and each of their sons and wives. Do you think this was just for practical purposes, so that the human race could repopulate the earth? Explain. What important truth might be communicated here about the connection between an individual finding the favor of God and that person's family?

How does verse 22 relate to verses 8 and 9?

Staying Faithful

Can you imagine the response Noah might have experienced from his family and his neighbors as he built the ark? This was no minor project that he completed in his spare time in his basement; the ark would have been visible to all, and its construction would have been a full-time occupation. Noah may have faced ridicule from many and perhaps even hostility from some; he would have been branded as a fool. From time to time, we hear the inspirational stories of men and women who commit to a divinely inspired task without regard for what others might think. There are people around us every day who quietly sense God's leading and then follow it; their goal is faithfulness and obedience, not popularity.

In what ways does our faithfulness to God and his design for our lives bring God's favor and blessing to the world? In what ways is our infidelity to God and his design for our lives harmful to the world, diminishing our own lives and those of the other creatures God has made?

One person who finds favor in God's eyes might not seem very significant in the face of calamity such as that described in Genesis 6. But through Noah and his family we see light at the end of the tunnel. What does this teach us about our own potential or that of our families to expose others to the favor of God?

Sharing God's Favor

When my dad was just a boy, he would go once a month with his own father to a nearby barber shop for a haircut. This establishment was not like the chain hair salons that are so common today. The owner, Bob, was the one who cut hair, and he lived with his family in a small house on the back of the lot. One day Bob invited my grandpa and father to church. They accepted the invitation, and now, almost eighty years later, my dad is still a part of that same congregation. Not long after retiring, Bob passed away. And the stories poured forth about the many people he had invited to church and shared with about the love of God. Bob was not a perfect man; he would have been the first to admit that. But the legacy of his faith is still expanding—three and four generations beyond his own.

God has high hopes for each of his children, and each of us has fallen far short of those hopes. In what ways has the level of wickedness of the world around us surpassed that of Noah's day?

Just as the flood led to a new creation, the living water of God can make a new creation inside each and every one of us. We are invited to share the good news of that opportunity with others, by the things we say and also by the way we live. How will you proclaim life to your family, friends, neighbors, co-workers, and anyone else who comes across your path—even if you might be misunderstood or ridiculed for it?

Application

The story of Noah illustrates pretty plainly a direct link between the favor of God and choosing to live righteously, blamelessly, and faithfully before him. This is not about somehow earning our salvation but about realizing that it is best to do things God's way. Others may not understand the choices we are making, but we are making them for an audience of One and not many. We also see how it is possible to be "conduits" of the favor of God to our families and even to the world. Noah was not perfect, and neither are we. But we study God's Word and seek the help of his Holy Spirit to learn what God expects and respond accordingly. Like Noah, we too can find favor in the eyes of the Lord. ■

L2

Abraham

Genesis 15:1–6; 18:1–15

Main Point

Like Abraham, we can experience God's favor by choosing to place our trust in God and his promises.

Background

Sarah and Abraham attempted to resolve the problem of her barrenness through all the measures at their disposal. The tension of this situation, however, could be resolved only through the word of the promising God. In fact, it was only Yahweh's promise that stood over against the hopelessness of Sarah's empty womb. Sarah laughed at God's promise, but this laugh was likely devoid of all humor. Her dry, sarcastic laugh was the sort that might come from us when we realize that somebody has played a cruel joke on us. Meanwhile, Yahweh's promise endured. The hopelessness and unrelieved tension of these two barren old people would finally be resolved when Sarah became pregnant and bore Isaac.

A Call and a Promise

Land and an heir were the twin centerpieces of God's call and promise to Abram (later called Abraham) and Sarai (later called Sarah). This promise appeared to be outrageous. Both Abram and Sarai had reached an age at which conception was no longer possible. Sarai was barren. In the cultural world of the Old Testament, childlessness was nearly always considered the fault of the woman. A wife was expected to produce children, that is, heirs to carry on the family name. A barren woman was subject to reproach and shame among other women and her husband's displeasure at home. Barrenness signaled hopelessness.

We often refer to the Bible as the Word of God because it expresses the will of God and the story of God and his creation, communicated divinely to us. Genesis 15:1 talks about "the word of the LORD" coming to Abram. To what did this refer? What does "the word of the LORD" mean in this case, and what differentiates it from the written Word of God?

In our text, we will see that God communicated his word to Abram in a vision. Is this still a way God communicates with human beings? Explain. In what other ways does God communicate his word to us? How can we be sure that it is the word of God we are hearing and not our own preferences, the suggestions of others, or even the voice of the enemy?

---

1. Read Genesis 15:1–6.

Why would the Lord need to encourage Abram here not to be afraid? What might Abram have feared at this point?

In Abram's day, having a household servant receive one's inheritance was the expected outcome for someone who had no children, but this was not God's plan for Abram. When have you felt that the likely outcome of a situation was somehow "less than" what God promised or intended? How did things turn out? What did you conclude in hindsight?

According to Genesis 15:6, what was the connection between Abram's belief and his righteousness? Was this a one-time thing for Abram, or was it true for his whole life? Is it true for *all* of God's children? Explain.

When have you maintained belief in something that seemed improbable or even impossible? Why were you able to do so?

In response to their inability to have children, Abram and Sarai took matters into their own hands. How does God continue to work for the good in our lives in spite of our actions that might not be in line with his will? Can the things we do ever thwart the accomplishment of God's will? Explain.

II. Read Genesis 18:1–15.

God's children in the Old Testament understood the appearance of an angel of the Lord to be a visit from God himself. At what point do you think Abraham realized that his visitors were heavenly in nature, and why? What might have tipped him off?

Abraham's response upon noticing three strangers near his tent was to extend immediate hospitality, which included the lengthy process of baking bread and slaughtering and cooking a calf. Such activity was considered a cultural "norm" in that society. Does God expect all of his children to show quick and generous hospitality to others? Abraham expressed that he would consider himself a recipient of the favor of his guests if they would stay for a meal. What is the connection between showing hospitality to others and finding the favor of God?

The Lord Keeps His Promises

God had repeated his promise again and again to Abraham—for fourteen years. After such a long wait, Sarah found the promise laughable. To conceive and bear a child at her advanced age would be like saying that the baby would be born in a geriatric ward and Medicare would pay the bills. This is another instance where we can struggle to understand God's response; the Lord didn't seem to mind Abraham's laughter at hearing that he would be a father in his old age (Genesis 17:17), but he did take issue with Sarah's response of laughter. There are different kinds of laughter; we might laugh out of joy, in response to something funny, out of nervousness, when seeing people get what we think are their "just deserts," or even when something seems preposterous or unbelievable.

It is in God's character to promise, and God keeps the promises he makes. If barrenness is a metaphor for hopelessness, then what might God's promise to Abraham and Sarah stand for? Why? When have you seen this to be true?

____

____

____

It might be said that faith and trust are synonyms for the cornerstone virtue of the relationship of human beings to God. Based on your study of Abraham and Sarah, describe what you understand as the connection between faith and trust and finding or experiencing the favor of God.

____

____

____

Faith in Action

We know that Abraham seemed to get impatient as he was waiting for the fulfillment of God's promise to him. Really, the promise did not come to fruition until the arrival of Abraham's descendant Jesus Christ many generations later. Abraham's belief may have been expressed in words at certain points, but its proof was seen in Abraham's actions. God told him to leave home and move to a strange land that would one day be occupied by his descendants, so he did. Some time after his son Isaac was born, God told him to sacrifice Isaac as a burnt offering; Abraham had knife in hand when the Lord told him to stop. Abraham's faith or belief was illustrated by what he did.

How has the Lord worked in your life through seasons of barrenness and hopelessness, despite times when you have grown impatient or misunderstood his will?

____

____

____

____

____

____

Application

The story of Abraham and Sarah has much to teach us about the favor of God. It is easy to grasp that certain things we might do or certain attitudes we might hold would be displeasing to God. But in the case of Abraham, the thing he "did" to find God's favor was believe what God said, to take God at his word. Abraham believed the Lord before seeing the actual results of what the Lord had promised him. We also see an element of mystery again. What was it that caused God to select Abraham out of all people to be the father of a great nation and, through Christ, the "father" of God's people? Like Abraham, we can choose to place our trust in God and his promises. ■

L3

Moses

Exodus 33

Main Point

Like Moses, we can do what God asks us to do in spite of our own limitations.

Background

Scholars use the term *theophany* to describe events such as Moses' encounter with God at the burning bush. A theophany is the appearance or manifestation of God to human beings. The God who called Moses acted in a manner atypical of gods. Yahweh actually conversed with Moses. Other gods might have appeared in dreams or visions, but Yahweh *talked* with Moses. That tells us something about Moses' status as the man who spoke face-to-face with God, even as it tells us that Yahweh is willing to talk and work with human beings—even fugitive members of an enslaved race. Moses' call was about Yahweh as much as it was about Moses. Yahweh is a God who hears slaves and who is "concerned about their suffering" (3:7). God had a ready answer to each of Moses' objections, and underneath each answer was the promise, "I will be with you."

The Founder of Israel's Faith

In a very real sense, Moses was the great founder of Israel's faith. To be sure, he did not invent this faith and its traditions. As a prophet, he carried God's revealing word to the people. Of course Moses was not the only prophet of Israel, but prior to the exodus the Israelite tribes were a loose association of clans that shared a common ancestor in Abraham. After the exodus and during the wilderness sojourn, Israel became a people—the people of God. Moses was the key figure in that transformation.

The Lord God and Moses simply talked with each other. What about us today? Could any of us ever aspire to have a simple conversation with the Lord? If someone told you that he or she heard the voice of God, how would you respond? How do we know when we are hearing God and not someone or something else? How is the favor of God experienced through two-way communication with him?

____

____

While Moses may have enjoyed his personal relationship with the Lord, God used that relationship for the benefit of the Israelites, to provide them leadership and direction. How does God still act to bless families, friends, and churches through his relationship with leaders in these groups? How do we know these leaders are hearing and following the leading of God?

____

____

____

I. Read Exodus 33:1–11.

Look at Genesis 12:1–3. What is similar about what God asked Abram (Abraham) to do and what he asked Moses to do here? What is different between these two calls? What had changed in the centuries that passed between the two calls?

What does it mean for a person or people to be "stiff-necked"? Why did the ancient Israelites fit this description? What are some other examples you can think of? How does being stiff-necked rob someone of experiencing the favor of God? When have you seen this happen?

II. Read Exodus 33:12–22.

Moses knew he had the favor of God because God had told him so (verse 12). Now Moses requested some tangible signs of that favor: for God to teach him the Lord's ways, for the presence of God to be with him, and to see God's glory. What does it mean to "see the glory" of God? Is it possible for us to do this? If so, how? How might our experience be different from that of Moses, and how might it be similar to it?

The Lord's statement in the last part of verse 19 could be seen as very encouraging if we are among those to whom he has chosen to show mercy and compassion. At the same time, it could be bad news for those to whom God has not chosen to show mercy and compassion. What do you think? Is it possible to know God's criteria for making this choice? If so, what are they? If not, why not?

Although the Bible tells of the anger and wrath of God, it makes it clear that love is the ultimate foundation for what God does (John 3:16). The Bible is also clear about God being unchanging (Malachi 3:6). Why are these facts, in combination, a tremendous blessing to us? Why is God's consistency an important "companion" to his love?

God Chose Moses

The Lord is the kind of God who sees and hears and is moved by what he sees and hears. In the case of the ancient Israelites, this meant that someone needed to go to Egypt to lead the people out of bondage and to the Promised Land. It was for Israel's sake that Moses was called. Recall that Moses was initially hesitant, disputing whether he was really the one to do this great work of service to God. Would the people believe him? He claimed that he lacked the public presence and the forceful speech necessary to command. Nevertheless, God chose Moses and was willing to work with this reluctant prophet and his self-proclaimed limitations. The further we get into the story of Moses, the less we read about Aaron, his brother and designated spokesperson, other than Aaron's work as head priest. Moses stepped up to the plate, and God did what God promised to do.

Looking back on your life, how can you see God's favor even at times that you were reluctant or unsure or (at least in your own mind) totally unprepared to do what he asked? What is the "balance" between our own efforts and the work of God when God has called us to do something?

Presence

Presence can be such a powerful thing, but sometimes it also brings a simple comfort and peace. I can be sitting in my recliner doing nothing besides flipping through television channels or surfing the Internet on my smart phone. If my wife is present in the room and basically doing her own thing—even if we just exchange a word or comment every once in a while—I tend to feel more relaxed and content. We enjoy just being in each other's company. I have many loved ones who have gone on to be with the Lord, and I think of how much I would enjoy (*will* enjoy!) just being in their presence again.

The Holy Spirit is perhaps the least-understood and therefore the least-discussed member of the Trinity. Among the Spirit's many wonderful aspects is the way he resides in believers as the very presence of Christ and the Father (John 14:15–20; Romans 8:9). Sure, it would have been neat to walk this earth when Jesus did. But his presence is with us now. How and when do you feel Christ's presence in your life?

____

____

It was the Divine presence that called Moses and enabled him to faithfully lead the Hebrews to the Promised Land. Maybe God is calling you to accomplish a task in his name. How have you felt God's power in his presence with you? How have you felt God's peace, contentment, and joy?

____

____

Application

The story of Moses contains more of the thread of mystery of finding God's favor. What did the Lord see in this man that caused him to call Moses as the first leader of the Israelites? Moses was a flawed human, just as each of us are. By his own assessment, he was a poor speaker—and oratorical skills are pretty important if you are going to lead millions of people. But in spite of his own limitations, and like Noah and Abraham before him, Moses was willing to do what God asked him to do. He ended up facilitating miracles, spoke with the Lord face-to-face, and was used by God to communicate the laws that governed the Israelites for hundreds of years. Perhaps it was knowing that God had promised his favor and his presence that made the difference for Moses. ■

L4

Mary

Luke 1:25–56

Main Point

As with Mary, our response to God's favor reveals our character.

Background

Mary was likely in her mid-teens when she became pregnant, but we must remember that the idea of a lengthy adolescence between childhood and adult life is a fairly recent and largely Western development. Mary became pregnant at an age when most women in her society married and began having babies. It was not her age that distinguished Mary; it was her obedience, courage, and faith. Mary and Joseph were "pledged to be married" or "betrothed," but this was more than a modern-day engagement. Galilean marriages included two "weddings." The first was a kind of public declaration of marriage; cohabitation came after the second ceremony. It seems likely that Mary and Joseph were in the period between these two points when the angel Gabriel visited.

"The God-Bearer"

In the earliest centuries of the church, Christians in the city of Alexandria, Egypt, began referring to Mary, Jesus' mother, by the use of the Greek word *theotokos*, meaning "the God-bearer." This was a way of saying that Jesus was God himself. The Alexandrian Christians continued to use the term *theotokos*, and Mary's stature in the eyes of ancient and medieval Christians continued to grow.

The angel Gabriel, who was sent by God to speak with Mary, visited Zechariah in the first part of Luke 1, and he is also mentioned in chapters 8 and 9 of the Book of Daniel in the Old Testament. Take a look at these other appearances of Gabriel. What is the connection between them and Gabriel's appearance to Mary? What is significant about this connection?

1. Read Luke 1:26–38.

The very first thing Gabriel told Mary was that she was highly favored and that the Lord was with her. We have the benefit of hindsight with respect to this conversation. We know what was in store for Mary, but at this point she did not, which helps us understand why she initially responded as she did. What could Mary have possibly imagined about the meaning of Gabriel's complimentary words to her? In what ways does being favored by God trump any favor we might receive from other people?

Mary expressed uncertainty about how the things Gabriel promised from God would come true. Zechariah, the recent recipient of a visit from Gabriel, also expressed uncertainty about the fulfillment of what Gabriel had told him—a promise that also related to a miraculous birth. Zechariah was "punished" by being made unable to speak until his child of promise was born (see Luke 1:5–20). Why the difference in Gabriel's response to Zechariah's question and his response to Mary's question?

Elizabeth, the wife of Zechariah, was a relative of Mary's (the KJV, an older translation, refers to them as cousins, but a better understanding of the original Greek term implies a less specific relationship). When Gabriel let Mary know that Elizabeth was also expecting a miraculous child, he told her that "no word from God will ever fail" (verse 37). Prior to the updated translation in 2011, the NIV rendered Gabriel's words as "nothing is impossible with God." As with the difference between "cousin" and "relative," this reflects what the NIV translators felt is a better understanding of the original Greek. Is there any significance to the difference between the two ways of translating Gabriel's words? Does the change alter the ultimate meaning of the message of this passage in any way? Explain.

II. Read Luke 1:39–56.

What things did the Holy Spirit reveal to Elizabeth when Mary came to visit? Why might Elizabeth's specific words have been particularly important to Mary at this time?

Elizabeth affirmed that Mary had believed God's promise about the baby Mary would be having. What if Mary had not believed what Gabriel had said and been accepting of it? Did God know beforehand what Mary's response would be? Did he force her to respond in that way? If she had refused or continued to hesitate, would he have found someone else? What was the role of Mary's free will in the exchange with Gabriel? What clues do we gain from this about Mary's opportunity to experience the favor of God?

Mary's "song" (verses 46–55) was in response to the visit from Gabriel, her conversation with her relative Elizabeth, and the anticipated miraculous birth of her son. But the words Mary spoke, which were inspired by the Holy Spirit, seemed to address much more than just the arrival of a baby. Knowing what we know now, how would Mary's child grow up to bring mercy to generations of people, change the balance of world power, and help the descendants of Abraham forever?

What are some possible reasons why Mary rushed to see her relative Elizabeth and then stayed with her for three months?

Highly Favored

By the end of our study text, Mary was prophetically praising God for what he had promised to do. But her first reaction to Gabriel's greeting was not trust; it was astonishment. After all, it was an angel who brought word to her of being favored by God. We like to think of angels almost as cuddly and mild beings, but their appearance would likely cause us to be startled or troubled. Mary needed to clearly understand her call from God to bear the Messiah. And all of us should seek to discern God's call and mission for our lives, however he should choose to communicate it.

Mary was probably in her mid-teen years, but she was open to God's action in her life in an extraordinary way. Do you feel that Mary's age was a distinguishing characteristic? How about her obedience, courage, and faith? What might this say to us about the faith of teenagers today and the distinguishing characteristics of our own faith?

____

____

The first two chapters of Luke's Gospel paint a very positive picture of Mary: she was favored by God, humble, obedient, believing, worshipful, and faithful to Jewish law. Do you think it was these qualities that "qualified" Mary to be chosen and favored by God, or was it simply the intent and purpose of God to choose her? Why do you say so?

____

____

____

The Favor of God's Plan

I grew up in church—Sunday school, morning worship, evening worship, Wednesday-night service, youth group, choir, skits and plays, swim parties, summer camp, conventions, the whole package. Yet it wasn't until I was seventeen years old or so that I really began to understand God's desire for me to live in full submission to him. I didn't come under this conviction during a church service or at any particular moment; the awareness seemed to grow on me until I became fully convinced of it. The older I get, the more I view the past events of my life within the larger purposes of God. Things that happened in my childhood, people I knew, places I worked or lived—it has all fit together beautifully to lead me to where I am today.

How has God worked in your life to enable you for the work he has for you?

Application

Today's passage—especially the portion known as Mary's "song" or poem—says a lot about Mary's character. Her praise to God had little to do with God's choice of her to be Jesus' mother. Mary humbly sang not about herself but about what God had done. And she expressed certainty about the fulfillment of what Gabriel had promised. Mary placed the events of her own life within the larger purposes of God. What God would do through her, Mary found to be consistent with what God had done in the past. Through her son Jesus, the Lord would raise the lowly and bring low the exalted. Mary was favored by God to be an integral part of the ultimate display of God's favor, which would be available to all people as Isaiah had prophesied. ■

L5

Jesus

Luke 2:22–52

Main Point

Jesus Christ made the abundant and eternal favor of God available to the world.

Background

The canonical Gospels do not tell Jesus' complete life story; two do not mention either his birth or childhood. In none of the four do we read anything like a modern biography that tries to explain in some detail the formative influences that shape a person's development. The Gospels were not written to provide extensive chronological details but so that people would have sufficient information about Jesus to come to saving faith in him. Luke's infancy narrative gives us a picture of a peaceful return to Nazareth with a brief pause in Jerusalem in order to fulfill legal requirements. Leviticus 12 governed the condition of uncleanness associated with childbirth. Completing the prescribed ritual cleansed the person and restored him or her to full participation in the community of Israel. Joseph and Mary followed these Levitical regulations, bringing Jesus to the temple to be circumcised and to offer a sacrifice of two doves in keeping with the prescribed rules.

Separate unto God

In many ancient cultures and in today's traditional cultures, the idea of ritual cleanness was and remains widely accepted. The ancient Israelites took very seriously God's statement, "Be holy because I, the LORD your God, am holy" (Leviticus 19:2). To be holy meant to be separate unto God, and ritual cleanness was one way of indicating that separation. The people who lived within this system of ceremonial cleanness and uncleanness did not view it as intrusive or burdensome—it was just the way things were.

Joseph and Mary followed the Levitical regulations by bringing the baby Jesus to the temple to be circumcised and to offer a sacrifice. What does this indicate about their commitment to the Law of God? What might it reveal to us about God's reasons for selecting Mary to give birth to Jesus and Joseph to serve as his earthly father?

I. Read Luke 2:22–39.

For a person to be "consoled" is to be comforted in her or his sorrow. In what ways, as a nation or people group, was Israel in need of consolation in Simeon's day? What did Simeon indicate about the reach of the salvation Jesus would provide?

In what ways has Jesus caused some people to "fall" and others to "rise"? In what ways do some people speak against Jesus, and why? How does Jesus reveal the thoughts of people's hearts? How would Mary's own heart be "pierced" with sorrow?

Anna affirmed the salvation and redemption Simeon had prophesied that Jesus would bring. Why would the favor of God be necessary for anyone to accomplish what Jesus was sent to do?

Simeon and Anna were faithful Jews—aged servants of God who watched as Mary and Joseph and the infant Jesus fulfilled the Law's requirements and expressed their hope in the coming Messiah. At only eight days old, Jesus was already being revealed to the world. What extent of understanding do you think Simeon and Anna had about the things they prophesied concerning Jesus, and why? After hearing what Simeon and Anna said, what do you think Mary and Joseph anticipated about Jesus' future and the role he would play? Why?

II. Read Luke 2:41–52.

Joseph and Mary made the trek to Jerusalem annually for the Passover. Not all Jews did this, so this fact helps us to see that Jesus was reared as a true son of Israel. At every milestone of their son's life, Mary and Joseph faithfully discharged their responsibilities as Jewish parents. Age twelve was a significant moment for Jesus to be back in the temple: the age of *bar mitzvah*, the time when a Jewish child becomes a son or daughter of the covenant and is considered to be an adult (for girls the term is *bat mitzvah*). When you were twelve, in what ways did you exhibit adult tendencies, and in what ways were you still a child? What were your awareness of God and spiritual life like at that point? To what level do you think twelve-year-olds are able to know and experience the favor of God? What might it look like in their lives?

When Jesus' distraught parents found him talking theology with the rabbis and learned sages of Israel, he asked them if they realized that he needed to be about his Father's work. Although Mary and Joseph had been visited by an angel, had experienced the miracle birth of Jesus, had heard the prophesies of Simeon and Anna, and had raised Jesus in the faith of Israel, why do you think they were still mystified by Jesus' question? What encouragement should this give us in our own process of spiritual growth?

What does it mean to "treasure" something in your heart? How is it possible to treasure even an incident of conflict or anxiety or something we do not understand?

Growing in Favor

Even before Jesus' birth, signs and miracles attended his life. At the proper moment, his parents had presented him in the temple. Now, at age twelve, it was time for Jesus to honor—by his own decision—all the indicators and expressions of faith that had been made for him. It is clear that he was already beginning to have some understanding of his role in life, though he wouldn't launch his public ministry until he was around thirty. For any of us, God's timing and the fulfillment of his plan for our preparation are key to stepping up and stepping out "at the proper moment."

What things might Jesus have done to grow in wisdom and in favor with other people? Was his increasing favor with God something he took steps to obtain, or did it simply result from the fact that he was the Son of God? What role might Jesus' obedience have played? From the previous weeks' studies, what similarities and differences do you see between the favor of God as experienced by other biblical characters and the favor of God as experienced by Jesus?

The incident at the temple would not be the last time a saying of Jesus left his hearers puzzled. Now that he had owned the mission God had called him to, how and why did tension rise between Jesus and those who did not understand his words? How does such tension rise even today?

Blessed to Be a Blessing

"You are blessed to be a blessing!" Many years ago my wife and I attended an Old Testament Bible seminar at our church, and that's the way the teacher summarized God's call to Abraham. It really is a great way to describe the theme of the Scriptures as a whole. Yes, the Bible tells us how to have a relationship with God through Jesus Christ. But we live that relationship out by loving others and sharing with them how they, too, might have such a relationship. One part of the beauty of the body of Christ is the give-and-take nature of the fellowship. When everyone contributes their time, talents, and resources, there is plenty to go around.

Our blessings from the Lord are designed to be shared. When have you given of your time, talents, and resources to benefit the body of Christ? When have you found yourself in need and been blessed by the gifts of others?

____

____

"Every good and perfect gift is from above, coming down from the Father of the heavenly lights, who does not change like shifting shadows" (James 1:17). Use the space below to express your gratitude to God for the blessings in your life.

____

____

Application

It is pretty natural for us to put the favor Jesus received from God in a class of its own, and in some ways we may be right to do this. But one important aspect of that favor was its purpose. It was God's plan for Jesus to "share the wealth" and he did so abundantly, as the words of many classic hymns and contemporary praise choruses passionately proclaim. It was through Jesus Christ that the abundant and eternal favor of God was made available to all. The "year of the Lord's favor" that Isaiah talked about? Jesus ushered it in. And the timeframe was not limited to a literal year—it is forever. All that went before in the course of human history pointed to this, and the world would never be the same. ■

L 6

Favor versus Favoritism

Acts 10:1–23, 34–43; Romans 2:11–16

Main Point

The favor of God is nothing we could ever earn or deserve; God bestows it because he loves us.

Background

Jesus' life and ministry occurred largely among the Jewish people; the first Christians were Jewish and assumed that Jesus was the Messiah of Israel. That he was also the Lord of the Gentiles was an idea that took the church a while to accept. Through Simon Peter's encounter with a Gentile believer, Peter realized that God "accepts from every nation the one who fears him and does what is right" (10:35). The church was being called to embrace the whole world and not limit its work to Israel alone. Paul's Letter to the Romans expresses an understanding that God's righteousness is available to all people. In the opening chapter, Paul included a capsule version of the gospel and the contents of the letter's main body. Because this gospel is based on salvation through faith and not works or heritage, it truly is good news to all.

So All Might Be Saved

Ever since the tower of Babel led to the division of human beings according to language, cultural and ethnic differences have played a large role in human relations. In many cases, ethnic difference is employed to demean, suppress, and even destroy. Jews and Judaism followed the ancient world's pattern of ethnocentrism. By the era of the New Testament, Jews maintained a strict separation between themselves and Gentiles, but their ethnocentrism added its own theological rationale to the standard attitudes of ethnic superiority. Jews pointed to God's covenants with Abraham and Moses as signs that God had chosen them and that they were therefore special. God had indeed chosen Israel, but as the means through which all peoples might be saved, not so the Israelites could consider themselves superior to others.

Why do you think God chose Cornelius, a Gentile, to have a vision instructing him to make contact with Simon Peter, a Jew? What might this indicate about God's communication with or revelation to those who sincerely seek God?

I. Read Acts 10:1–23, 34–43.

Many parents worry that their children will be "pulled down" by spending time with friends of questionable character. In your opinion, how does it work? Do "good" kids help "bad" kids be good, or do the "bad" kids influence the "good" kids to be bad? How does it work for us as adults? How does it work in a marriage? Would God fault us for trying to avoid people we think might lead us to sin? Explain.

How does verse 23 indicate that Peter already understood the meaning of the vision he had just had?

In your opinion, is favoritism always bad? Don't we all show favoritism—for example, by favoring family members or friends over strangers? Peter said that God does not show favoritism, so what is the difference between that and God showing *favor* to someone? Aren't there examples of times when God showed favoritism—for example, by choosing the offering of Abel over that of Cain or choosing Jacob over Esau? Was Peter just talking about favoritism with respect to salvation here, or was his statement inclusive of all kinds of situations? Explain.

What does it mean to "fear" God? We have all sinned and fallen short of God's standard (Romans 3:23), so how can any of us say that God accepts us because we do what is "right"? What does it mean to do what is right in God's eyes?

How would you summarize the message Peter shared with the crowd gathered at Cornelius's house? How did it make clear the abundant favor of God and also the fact that God does not show favoritism?

II. Read Romans 2:11–16.

Based on the text from Romans 2, what would you say is the relationship between God's Law and sin? If sin leads to death and we are saved by faith in Christ (Romans 6:23), then what is the role of obedience with respect to our faith? What (if any) portions of the Old Testament Law are we to obey, and why?

Describe a time in your life when it was clearly revealed to you that the law of God (the all-encompassing will of God even beyond the Old Testament Law) was "written" on your heart. What brought you to this realization? How did you respond, and what were the results in the end?

Considering your life right now, are there any areas or relationships in which you are showing favoritism that is wrong? How does the way God has shown you favor without favoritism encourage you to make a change in these areas or relationships? How can the Holy Spirit help to bring about the needed changes?

Double Conversion

Cornelius already had some knowledge of God, but he needed to be converted to "the Way" (Acts 9:2 records the first instance of Christianity being described with this term). Peter, although already a disciple of the Lord Jesus, needed to be converted to the realization that the gospel is for both Jews and Gentiles. In Acts 10, we see that God acted to bring an "outsider" with limited knowledge to the truth and also worked to help an "insider" understand that he still had some things to learn. God is at work in contexts and ways we don't always understand and may not even be aware of. We can be his agents to share his truth even as we continue to grow in our understanding of that truth.

The first Christians were Jewish. It made sense to them that Jesus would be the Messiah of Israel, and they had difficulty accepting the fact that Gentiles could be saved, as well. Describe a time when you showed favoritism, only to realize at some point that you were wrong. How was the truth revealed to you, how did you change course, and how did others respond?

The revelation Peter had from his dream and his encounter with Cornelius showed him that the gospel was not the private property of the Jews and that the church would need to embrace the whole world instead of limiting its work to Israel alone. How do churches sometimes fall into the trap of doing ministry as if the gospel were their "private property"?

Favor, not Favorites

Proverbs 22:6 states, "Start children off on the way they should go, and even when they are old they will not turn from it." Traditional teaching has seen this verse as a guarantee that children raised in the Christian faith will embrace that faith as adults. But some people suggest that to "start children off on the way they should go" is not limited to matters of faith. Of course every child should be raised to know of God's love and how to experience a relationship with the Lord, but the rest of "the way" we raise children should vary depending on their individual personalities, temperaments, and gifts. One set of parents' "ways" may look different for each of their children. Treating different children in different ways doesn't necessarily indicate favoritism.

Our loving Creator knows each of us better than we know ourselves. He sees the darkness within us and the sin that separates us from him, yet by his favor he has made a remedy for that darkness and provided a way back to him. No "favorites" in this plan—just the free gift of salvation and an endless list of other blessings to boot. How has your view of the favor of God changed as a result of this study?

Application

The favor of God is a mysterious and wonderful and persistent thing. It can have a variety of purposes—to show us the best way to live, to bless those around us, to help us lead others or fulfill a certain task. Nothing limits our potential to experience the joy of God's favor—not age or lack of experience or gender or ethnicity or anything else. We can assuredly say that God delights in bestowing his favor upon people and that he shows it without favoritism. It was God's plan all along to make his favor available to everyone, and in the fullness of time he did so (Galatians 4:4–7). So let us humbly ask God for his favor and seek it and knock on the door of heaven. "For everyone who asks receives; the one who seeks finds; and to the one who knocks, the door will be opened" (Luke 11:10). ■